The Frugal Florist™

Do-it-Yourself Flowers on a Budget

by
John Klingel AIFD
with Susan Baker

AuthorHouse™
1663 Liberty Drive, Suite 200
Bloomington, IN 47403
www.authorhouse.com
Phone: 1-800-839-8640

First published by AuthorHouse 6/11/2007

ISBN: 978-1-4343-0837-5 (sc)

Library of Congress Control Number: 2007903119

Printed in the United States of America
Bloomington, Indiana

This book is printed on acid-free paper.

authorHOUSE®

Dedication

This book is dedicated to my friend and closest advisor, Vincent C. Petrovsky, AIFD. Friends like Vince, with their unconditional love and support, help all of us achieve goals we never thought possible.

I love you, Vince,

John

Contents

Acknowledgments

Photography by Robin Nelson

The Cloisters Townhomes, Lake Worth, Florida

Pam and Andy at Kobosko's, West Palm Beach, Florida

Color wheel provided by Design Master Color Tool Inc., www.dmcolor.com

Foreword

So many people are convinced that they have no talent when it comes to arranging flowers. I say, "Not so!" I've spent more than thirty-three years teaching floral design, and every student says the same thing: "This wasn't as hard as I thought!" or "I didn't know I had it in me!"

Anyone who can follow basic step-by-step instructions can create a beautiful flower arrangement. The secret is to start with a simple design, then build on experience—and I'm going to show you how.

The most important part of my job is giving encouragement to the student who wants to learn. Our minds limit what we do before we even try. This book gives you information on how to buy flowers, follow my easy instructions, and create something beautiful. In the end, you'll be amazed at what you've accomplished—and I guarantee that you'll have fun along the way.

Flowers have played a role in human civilization dating back to as early as 2500 BC. When archaeologists explored the tombs of the Egyptian pharaohs, they discovered evidence that flowers—primarily water lilies and papyrus—were used in garlands as part of the ceremony for sending the departed on to their next life.

In today's modern world, we can purchase flowers almost anywhere, for virtually any occasion or no occasion at all. Whatever the reason, there is a personal connection that reflects the buyer's feelings and intentions. Sure, the flowers alone are beautiful and evoke an emotional response. But when blossoms are arranged, they have more value, meaning, purpose, and appreciation.

When ancient people began paying attention to the moon's cycle and realized the changing seasons repeated over and over again, a calendar was formulated. Once this tracking system was in place, people were able to celebrate important occasions on the same day each year. In our culture today, we arrange flowers to express a sentiment, celebrate life's special moments, or just bring color and joy into our home.

I consider floral design a three-dimensional art form that incorporates the elements and principles of design. Combine those elements and principles with good floral mechanics, and the result is a beautiful arrangement. Designing flowers provides instant gratification. While painting and sculpting demand hours or days worth of time, an arrangement of flowers can be completed in just a few minutes. By combining nature's own color palate with a few simple tips, your floral design can express your feelings or change someone else's.

Introduction

Many have asked me, why did you write this book? The answer is in three words: flowers are everywhere! We now have access to more flowers in more places than ever before. The grocery stores, discount clubs, convenient stores, produce stands, drug stores and even the gas stations have gotten in on selling flowers.

The bouquets are usually cello wrapped combinations of long-lasting blossoms with little or no design quality. This is where *The Frugal Florist* comes in; focusing on primarily the varieties of flowers that are available in mass markets.

It's important to understand that what a professional, retail florist provides is different from what most mass marketers provide. Much like going to a restaurant and enjoying the dining experience, the consumer calls the florist for their services which are mainly design talent and delivery. We all know that you can buy food for a lot less in the grocery store than what is served in most restaurants; it's the same with flowers.

Many of you "flower lovers" desire the creative experience in designing the arrangement yourself. And doing what we call in the industry, "the chop-and-plop" in a vase isn't your style. That was the motivation for writing *The Frugal Florist*, sharing a book of ideas and simple instructions on what to do with those mass market flowers. Yes, the flowers are beautiful but when you add "your touch" that makes them even more special.

As you turn though the pages of this book you will find simple ideas that you can recreate just by following the instructions, diagrams and photos.

Remember what you design is your own creation. Be proud of your accomplishment and as long as you had fun doing it you are successful.

So, buy flowers often, visit www.frugalflorist.biz for design kits and floral accessories, have fun and you will become *The Frugal Florist*.

Chapter 1 -
Identifying and Selecting Quality Flowers

With just a few easy pointers, you will be able to determine which flowers are fresh and which aren't. First, check the condition of the water the flowers are stored in. If the water is green and smells bad, the flowers have been exposed to bacteria and will not last. Next, pull the cellophane or paper wrapping down and look closely at the stems and leaves. If they are yellow, brown, and moldy, moisture has rotted the stems, and water will not travel up to the head. This is especially true in roses. Look at the flower blossoms. Do they appear fresh and undamaged? Flowers should be firm and free of any insects, broken heads, and black spots.

If the flowers appear slightly withered or dehydrated, cut the stems approximately one inch from the bottom of the stem and place in clean, room-temperature tap water. Allow them to drink for at least one hour before arranging.

In designing the arrangements in this book, I created a basic paint-by-number format in which I suggest which flowers to buy. Using The Frugal Florist—Flower Diagrams, you can also select the flowers you want to create any design style. While there are many blossoms to choose from, I have placed those into four categories—round or mass, spike or linear, filler or accent, and form flowers—to make the choices easier for you. A diagram accompanying each design shows where to insert each flower in the floral foam or grid. If you can't find a particular flower, simply substitute another flower in that group. And remember, it's not necessary to use flowers in all four groups. You can use any combination of flowers you like. Be creative!

Caring for your finished arrangements is very important.

Flowers respond to temperatures and conditions much the same way we do. Keep finished arrangements away from extreme heat or cold, direct sunlight or ceiling fans. These conditions dry out flowers more quickly. Always keep the container full of water. I advise adding a floral preservative if it's available. Change the water in a vase if it turns green or smells bad. You can add a half cap of bleach per gallon of water to prevent bacteria from developing.

Round or Mass

Spike or Linear

2

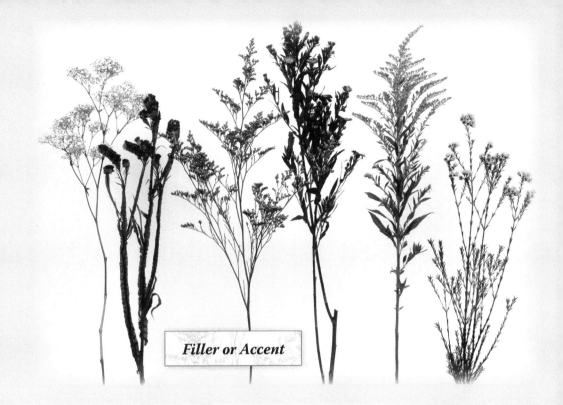

Filler or Accent

Form Flower

3

The Frugal Florist-Flower Diagrams

Flower Form Descriptions:

Round or Mass:
Generally flowers with a single
head use to create a focal point
and depth in the design.
Examples pictured left to right: a rose, sunflower, daisy, carnations, tulip, spray mums

Spike or Linear:
Flowers that grow tall with a
resemblance of a blade and used
for the outline of a design.
Examples pictured left to right: a gladioli, delphinium, larkspur, snap dragon, liatris,
Bells of Ireland, orchid spray

Filler or Accent:
Small, light and airy flowers that
fill in spaces and are used to soften
the arrangement.
Examples pictured left to right: baby's breath, statice, limonium, September flower,
solidago, wax flower

Form:
Independent blossoms that become
dominate in the design and require
their own space to draw attention.
Examples pictured left to right: alstroemeria, Asiatic lily, bird-of-paradise, ginger,
anthurium, heliconia

Chapter 2 -
Mechanics

There are basically three types of floral design mechanics: floral foam, a taped or wire grid laid over the container opening, or a pin holder, which is sometimes referred to as a pin frog.

Many of the arrangements shown in this book are designed in wet floral foam. The foam acts like a sponge, soaking up water. The foam can be re-watered, but reusing it is not recommended. Remember, never force the foam underwater, fill the sink and place the foam on the water's surface and allow it to gradually soak-about 20 seconds-however, colored foam can take up to 5 minutes. Flowers should be inserted as deeply as possible into the floral foam. Heavier stems especially should be deeply inserted, to properly secure them. Flowers cut on an angle go into the foam better. The foam can be cut to fit a basket liner, glass bowl, or plastic dish, and secured with waterproof tape. These products can be purchased at www.frugalflorist.biz.

Occasionally, wire mesh, or chicken wire, purchased from a hardware store, is used over the opening of a container as a mechanic to hold the flowers in place. A square piece of wire mesh can be loosely shaped into a ball and placed over the container opening. Make the ball-shape of the wire larger than the opening of the container, so it doesn't fall inside. Then, simply insert your stems through the openings of the wire mesh.   Adding foliages and filler flowers will cover the wire mesh mechanic.

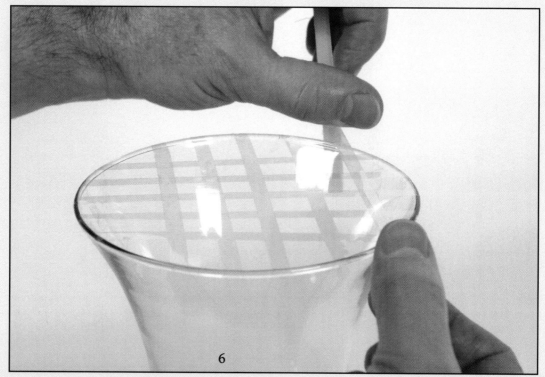

Chapter 3 -
Guide to Right Container

It has been said that the container makes the arrangement—not necessarily. Although an arrangement coordinated with the appropriate container can make a statement. Here we are focusing on, for the most part, inexpensive containers. As we say in the industry, put the value into the flowers. The container mainly serves as a reservoir so the flowers have a water source and something to hold them together.

The form or shape of the arrangement often follows the shape of the container, such as: tall, flared vase designs require a flared vase; cylindrical vases create strong vertical arrangements, and long and low arrangements work best in rectangular trays or round bowls.

The Frugal Florist suggests inexpensive plastic, glass, or baskets as containers. Illustrated here are some of the basic container shapes and the styles of arrangements that are best suited to them. As a general rule of thumb, a one-sided arrangement should be at least one and a half to two-times the height of the container. If the arrangement is round, the flowers should be at least two-thirds the size of the container. However, this can vary some, depending on where you are going to place the finished arrangement.

You can also place the inexpensive container inside of a pretty dish or crystal bowl lined with aluminum foil. If the outer container is too deep, you can elevate the arrangement's container on a piece of Styrofoam or invert a smaller bowl inside.

Shape of arrangement	Suggested container style

round mound   tray   low bowl

long and low   rectangle dish   tray   low bowl

one sided   rectangle dish   low bowl   pedestal

vase arrangement   flared vase   cylinder   ginger jar

The flowers are part of the dining experience and should not block the view of those sitting opposite you. The one exception to this is when the table seats twelve or more and is substantial in size. Guests generally do not shout across the table at someone. They tend to keep conversations between the people seated next to them. Tall arrangements can be placed against a wall or backdrop. If you have chosen a basket or metal bucket as your container, a heavy-duty garbage bag will work as a liner. Simply cut the plastic to fit the container and hold the floral foam and water.

Groupings of small arrangements can be very effective. Use small vases that take one or two blossoms, and arrange the vases together in the table center to complete one floral design composition. This idea works great when you have some leftover blossoms.

Chapter 4 -
How to Tie the Perfect Bow

Bows can evoke a mood. Gold and white ribbon, for example, can be elegant and sophisticated. Gingham ribbons represent a country or whimsical look. Holiday designs are often accented with velvet or pattern ribbons. Bridal flowers represent romance, so they are often embellished with lace and satin ribbon. When flowers are presented as a gift, ribbon treatments dress the arrangement to look special.

So many people struggle with bow-tying. The secret to beautiful bows is practice, practice, practice. Of course, the easiest solution is to use a pull-bow, but perhaps you want to create a customized bow or ribbon treatment. It's really pretty simple. By following the diagram, you can easily fashion your own bow to any size you wish.

Start by holding the ribbon in between your thumb and index finger, leaving a piece of the ribbon long enough for a streamer. If the ribbon has a pattern, such as polka dots, keep the pattern facing you by giving the ribbon a half twist after each loop. As you loop the ribbon back and forth, make each set of loops bigger, until you get the desired size.

Take the last ribbon loop over your thumb to create the center of the bow, leaving another piece of the ribbon long enough for a streamer. You can add more streamers to the back of the bow. Use a floral wire, pipe cleaner, or another piece of ribbon to tie the gathered ribbon together as tight as possible. Shape the bow by pulling the loops side to side.

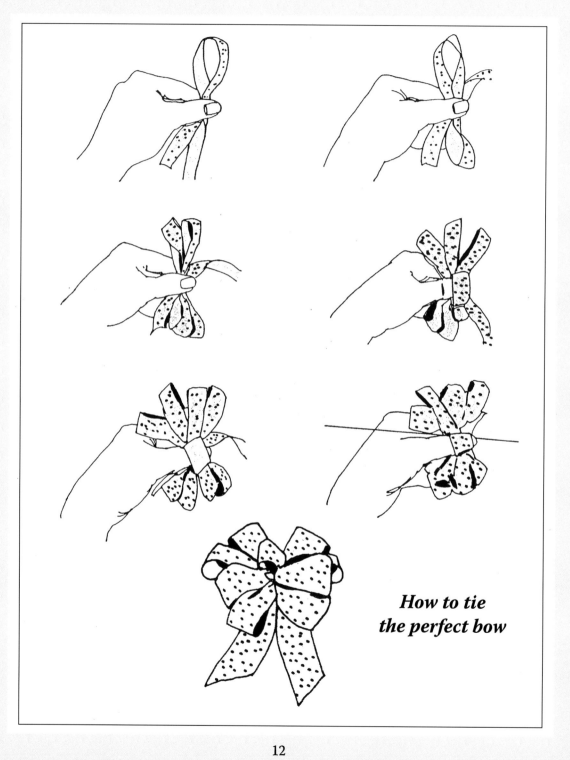

*How to tie
the perfect bow*

12

Chapter 5 -
Tools of the Trade

Your tools are an important part of creating a properly constructed floral arrangement. Some of the tools you will use are: a folding pocketknife, flower cutters, wire snips, and ribbon scissors. Tools can be purchased at a hardware store, garden center, or even your local supermarket.

Keep your tools clean by washing them in soap and warm water. Sharpen knives for an angled cut. Flowers respond best to water and floral foam when they are cut at a sharp angle. Never crush or smash the stems. Doing so will hinder the absorption of water up the stem.

THE COLOR WHEEL

The traditional color wheel has three primary colors: red, yellow, and blue. In technical terms, it organizes colors by the length of their light wave (red is the longest, violet is the shortest). But for those of us who aren't astrophysicists, it's easier to think of the color wheel as a slice of the rainbow stretched into a circle. Or maybe just a cool device that allows people to see the relationship between colors.

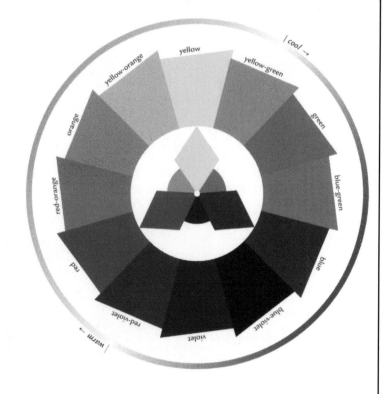

Chapter 6 -
Use of Color

I have a basic philosophy regarding flowers and colors: Flowers of all colors grow together in a garden. A floral design is a temporary gift that represents a sentiment or brightens up a room. Your food doesn't match the interior of your home, so fresh flowers don't need to match the interior of your home either. You give someone a dozen red roses to say "I love you," not because the person has a red living room!

Certain color combinations can create certain feelings. Warm, advancing colors such as red, orange, and yellow are stimulating and aggressive. Cool, receding colors, such as blue, green, or violet, are calming and soothing. Yellow evokes cheer, while red or hot pink represents passion, and white suggests respect or reverence. The primary colors of red, yellow, and blue are considered juvenile. Light blue is associated with baby boys, while pink is for baby girls.

While you can refer to the color wheel for guidance on selections, color trends in wedding flowers are governed by fashion and of course the bride's favorites. While white and cream are still favorites for traditional bridal bouquets many first-time and encore brides are selecting bright, contrasting colors, especially for those outdoor wedding celebrations that are on a beach or in a garden. Remember to select contrasting colors to the bridesmaids dresses so the flowers stand out in the pictures.

The Color Wheel is provided compliments of **Design Master, Inc.**

Chapter 7 -
Elements and Principles of Design

When learning about design of any kind, it's important to have a clear definition of the Five Elements of Design. They are: **line, space, form, color, and texture.** When well-represented in a design, these elements create a total/overall look that is aesthetically pleasing.

Without **line**, we would not have a path for the eye to follow. **Space** is the interruption between the other elements. **Form** is the shape of the end result. **Color** is the element that draws the most immediate response. **Texture** gives visible character to the design's surface structure. These elements, when used properly, can send a message, create a mood, or generate a thought.

In addition, there are also seven main principles of design. They are: **accent, balance, composition, harmony, proportion, unity,** and **rhythm**. Even in the most simple of floral arrangements, these principles are applied to create an end result that everyone who sees it can enjoy.

Every design is accented by a color, pattern, or motif. Visual or physical **balance** creates stability, making the arrangement solid in its placement. Often, a symmetrical balance is preferred over an asymmetrical balance. The **composition** of different materials pulls together a unified look that produces the desired effect. **Harmony** is achieved when all the parts of a design used together communicate a feeling of contentment. It's important that the **proportion** or comparative size relationships of the ingredients in the design are pleasing to the eye, and that the scale of the completed arrangement fits into the designated space.

Unity produces a single, general effect in our floral composition that can represent purpose and style. A **rhythm** of motion that is visual is achieved as the eye moves through the arrangement of flowers and foliage. There can also be a physical rhythm if the flowers and foliages move in the breeze or bounce while being transported.

It's not necessary for you to have great natural talent to create an attractive floral arrangement. "The Frugal Florist" is a simple approach to creating such arrangements. With the help of my detailed step-by-step instructions and the accompanying diagrams and pictures, you can arrange a few varieties of flowers into a professional look. You only need to add your talent and personality to the process. Have fun with the flowers and remember that the arrangement is an expression of your creativity. Whether you made the floral design for yourself or as a gift, take pride in knowing that you did it! Remember, the more you practice, the better you'll get. Enjoy the experience! Accept the praise!

Chapter 8 –
Foliages from Your Garden

Foliage accents the flowers in your arrangement and hides the mechanics while the freshness of green brings out the colors. Many arrangements of just foliages have a great appeal, especially to men, reminding them of a lush garden or rainforest. Since greenery comes in colors too, such as gray and silver tones, yellow-green, blue-green, and variegated colors and patterns, you can experiment with many of the foliages suggested in this chapter.

The foliages featured in this book are generally available at your local market; however, there are alternatives to those. If you live in a temperate, tropical, or subtropical climate, there are many types of foliage available in your garden, such as mini-umbrella plant, croton, pittosporum, flat fern, palms, Eugenia, sprengeri fern, ming fern, plumosus, ivy, pothos, podocarpus, ligustrum, eucalyptus, liriopi, and many others.

Foliages that are available in a cold climate are boxwood, evergreens, galax leaves, camellia, huckleberry, myrtle, holly, and a large variety of ferns.

I would recommend cutting the mature foliage, which is darker in color, over the lighter-color new growth. The mature foliage lasts longer and is hardier. You can test the foliage by placing a piece of it in a cup of water for thirty minutes. If the foliage wilts, it will not hold up in your arrangement. Remember to keep the foliage away from direct sunlight, heat, or extreme cold.

Have fun with the foliage available to you by mixing them with other textures such as moss, stones or pebbles, marbles, and crystals. The natural elements, water and fire, can evoke many feelings when combined with beautiful foliages.

Chapter 9 -
Woven Palm Leaf

If you have done any knitting or made pot holders, this is an easy job for you.

Use any palm frond that has thin leaves, such as Tepe or Areca, and start at the bottom. Turn under the leaf and go under the next leaf above it. Follow over the next leaf and under the next, until the leaf is woven through. Repeat the process with the other leaves on the frond. The last leaf woven in will hold all of the others in place. Tie the leaves at the top with string.

To weave the opposite side, turn the frond over and repeat the process, this time turning the leaf over and under until the leaf is woven through. Tie all of the leaves together at the top with string.

Woven palm leaves can be used in arrangements and as placemats. They also make a fun giveaway at the end of a dinner party.

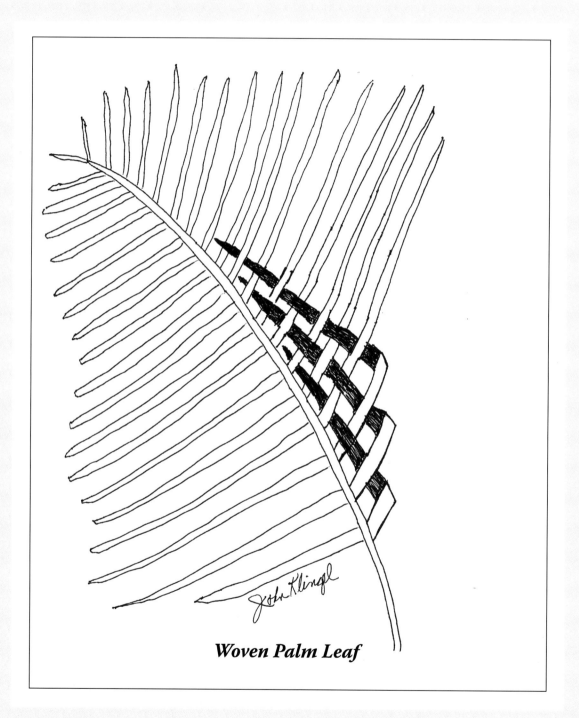

Woven Palm Leaf

Chapter 10 -
Colors of Roses and What they mean:

Red roses say "I love you." They also stand for respect and courage.

White roses say "You're heavenly." They also mean reverence and humility, innocence and purity, secrecy and silence.

Red and white roses together signify unity.

Pink roses symbolize grace and gentility. Deep pink stands for gratitude, appreciation, thanks.

Light pink roses convey admiration or sympathy.

Yellow roses stand for joy, gladness, and freedom and friendship.

Orange or coral roses denote enthusiasm and desire.

Red and yellow roses together stand for jovial, happy feelings.

Pale-colored roses convey sociability and friendship.

Rose buds symbolize beauty and youth or "you are young and beautiful."

Red rose buds mean "pure and lovely."

A single rose stands for simplicity. In full bloom means "I love you" or "I still love you."

Sweetheart roses symbolize just what their name implies.

Two roses taped together to form a single stem indicate an engagement or coming marriage.

Colors of Roses

Chapter 11 -
"Say It with Flowers" Tabletop Centerpiece

Dress up your table for a dinner party—or any other special occasion—with this dome-shaped arrangement of alstroemeria lilies. Choose flowers that match your home's color scheme, and accent the arrangement with an organic element such as Spanish moss or foliage from your garden.

To prepare the container, soak the floral foam in water, never forcing the foam under the water. Place the foam on the surface and allow it to soak gradually, which takes about thirty seconds. Secure the foam with waterproof tape. When designing with fresh flowers in wet floral foam, insert each stem only once, as far as possible, into the foam. Removing and reinserting stems weakens the foam. Place the tall flowers in the center of the container to create the height. Remember, you want your guests to be able to see over the arrangement. Next, insert four stems around the rim to create the width, keeping the arrangement small enough for the place settings. Add the remaining flowers in between, and finally, place the fern or baby's breath into the foam. To care for it, add water to the top of the container and keep it at room temperature, out of direct sunlight.

Design Tip

If you want candlelight, place candlesticks around the arrangement, remembering that candles are only appropriate after 5 PM.

Floral Recipe:

"Say It with Flowers"
Tabletop Centerpiece

Chapter 12 -
Bridal Shower Front-Door Wreath

Here comes the bride! Spread the joy of the wedding to your front door by welcoming shower guests with this lovely wreath. To establish the wedding's color scheme, use flowers in the favorite colors of the bride, and complement them with ribbon that matches the bridesmaids' dresses.

Fill a sink with water and place the wet foam wreath ring face down on the surface of the water, allowing it to soak completely. This will take about two minutes. Remove the wreath from the sink, and place it foam-side-up on a tabletop. Cut and place the fern into the foam in small pieces around the wreath. Cut the flower stems to approximately three inches, and place them around the wreath, keeping the space as even as possible in between the flowers. Add the baby's breath and ribbon, and display on the door using a wreath hanger or nail.

Design Tip

Use a sheer ribbon with a satin ribbon, or a pattern ribbon with a solid color for added interest. Attach the wreath to the door using the ribbon or a wreath hanger.

Floral Recipe:

Budget:
12 carnations (round)
6 stems baby's breath (filler)
10 stems fern
ribbon
1 wet foam wreath ring

Bridal Shower Front-Door Wreath

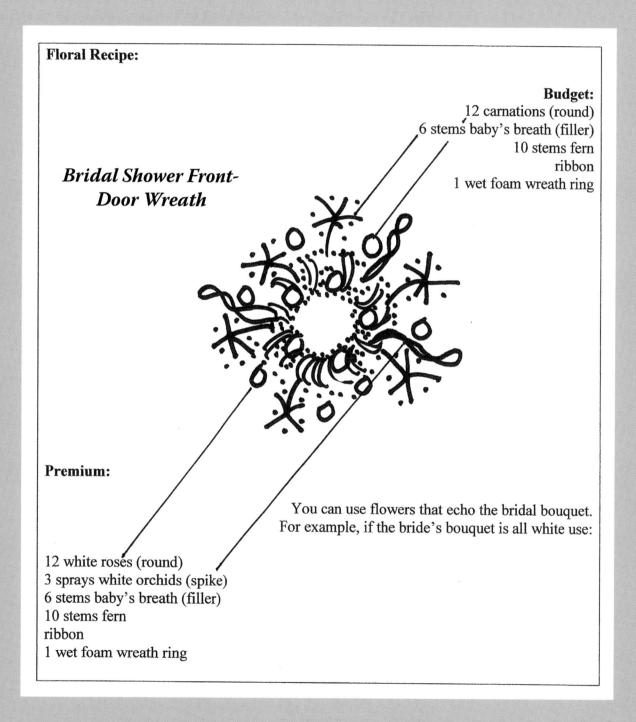

Premium:

You can use flowers that echo the bridal bouquet.
For example, if the bride's bouquet is all white use:

12 white roses (round)
3 sprays white orchids (spike)
6 stems baby's breath (filler)
10 stems fern
ribbon
1 wet foam wreath ring

Chapter 13 -
Circular Candle Centerpiece

Create a romantic setting for an anniversary party or wedding celebration with flowers and candlelight. A feast for the eyes is an important part of the dining experience, and shows your guests how much you care. Have a fun get-together with your bridal party the day before to create this lovely and simple arrangement to place on the table.

Fill a sink with water and place the wet foam wreath ring face down on the surface of the water, allowing it to soak completely. This will take about two minutes. Remove the wreath from the sink and place it foam-side-up on a tabletop. Cut and place the fern into the foam in small pieces around the wreath. Cut the flower stems to approximately three inches, and place them at random around the wreath, keeping the space as even as possible in between the flowers. Add the baby's breath or limonium and place the candle, candle holder, and hurricane shade in the center of the ring.

Design Tip

Instead of a taper candle and holder, use a pillar or jar candle. Hurricane shades or jar candles are needed for outdoor parties, and are suggested to contain the candle flame.

Floral Recipe:

Budget:

2 cello wrapped bunches of mixed flowers (round)
6 stems fern
1 wet foam ring
1 glass candle hurricane shade
1 candle holder
1 taper candle

Circular Candle Centerpiece

Premium:

12 roses favorite color (round)
6 stems fern
6 stems baby's breath or limonium (filler)
1 wet foam ring
1 glass candle hurricane shade
1 candle holder
1 taper candle

Chapter 14 -
"I Do, I Do" Hand-tied bouquets

Every girl dreams about her wedding day and the beautiful bouquet she'll carry down the aisle. When flowers are being used for a one-day event like a wedding, they must be allowed to develop, to show their full color.

Start with a center flower, and angle the additional flowers in a spiral pattern. If you are using a hydrangea bloom, work the roses in between the buds. Remember to keep the stems going in the same direction. Stems are flexible and will bend into place. The fragile part of the stem is just below the flower head, and can break easily if stressed. The stems can be bound together at the binding point just beneath the bouquet with twine, string, or ribbon.

Design Tip

Add trails of ivy that can be cut from a plant to the finished bouquet for a lovely cascade.

Floral Recipe:

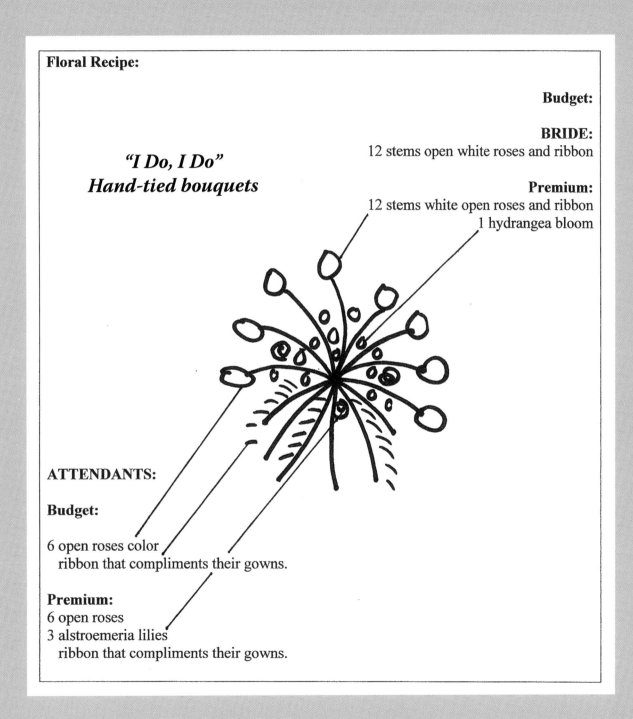

"I Do, I Do"
Hand-tied bouquets

Budget:

BRIDE:
12 stems open white roses and ribbon

Premium:
12 stems white open roses and ribbon
1 hydrangea bloom

ATTENDANTS:

Budget:

6 open roses color
   ribbon that compliments their gowns.

Premium:
6 open roses
3 alstroemeria lilies
   ribbon that compliments their gowns.

Chapter 15 -
"Oh, Baby!" basket

The delicate flowers nestled in a white wicker basket say "Welcome home!" to a new mom and her bundle of joy. According to tradition, blue is used for baby boys and pink for baby girls, but what if it is twins or you are not sure? Then yellow is the perfect color.

Prepare the basket by soaking a piece of floral foam in a plastic liner and place it in a white wicker basket. Cut and place the flowers, starting with the tallest in the center and shorter around the sides. Fill in with remaining flowers and add fern and filler flowers in between the blossoms.

Floral Recipe:

"Oh, Baby!" basket

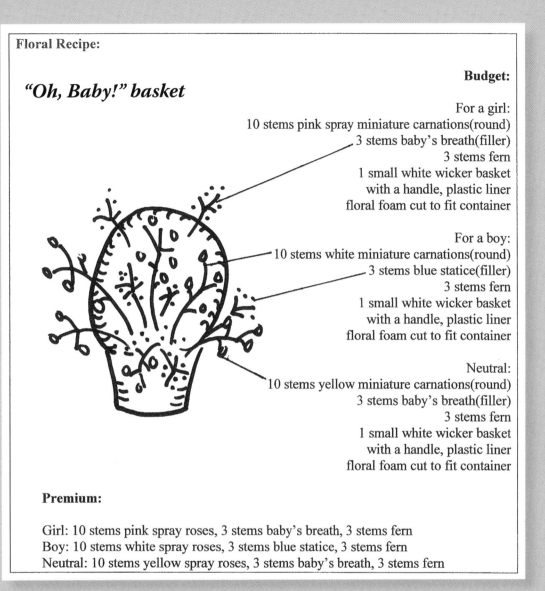

Budget:

For a girl:
10 stems pink spray miniature carnations(round)
3 stems baby's breath(filler)
3 stems fern
1 small white wicker basket
with a handle, plastic liner
floral foam cut to fit container

For a boy:
10 stems white miniature carnations(round)
3 stems blue statice(filler)
3 stems fern
1 small white wicker basket
with a handle, plastic liner
floral foam cut to fit container

Neutral:
10 stems yellow miniature carnations(round)
3 stems baby's breath(filler)
3 stems fern
1 small white wicker basket
with a handle, plastic liner
floral foam cut to fit container

Premium:

Girl: 10 stems pink spray roses, 3 stems baby's breath, 3 stems fern
Boy: 10 stems white spray roses, 3 stems blue statice, 3 stems fern
Neutral: 10 stems yellow spray roses, 3 stems baby's breath, 3 stems fern

Design Tip

Add rattles and pacifiers to the arrangement for a fun look.

Chapter 16 -
Gen-X bouquet

Every generation makes its mark and the Gen-X-er's are about color, color and more color. They adore all that's eye-catching -- bright greens, vivid yellows, and brilliant purples. Fun and funky design trends are what the Gen-X-er's look for such as flowers submerged under water and incorporating the use of decorative mechanics. What ever the design style is be sure to apply your creative edge that makes this arrangement take notice.

Start this bouquet with a contemporary-shaped container such as a cube or triangle. It can be a colored or clear, large or small. Simply add food coloring to the water to give a look that's wild and fun. Craft wire makes the perfect decorative mechanic. Just wrap it around the outside of the container, and then drop the flowers in between the wire frame.

Design Tip

Use colorful beads or crystals with the craft wire to embellish the arrangement.

Floral Recipe:

Budget:

3 stems green button mums(round)
2 stems yellow altroemeria lily(form)
3 stems purple statice(filler)

Gen-X bouquet

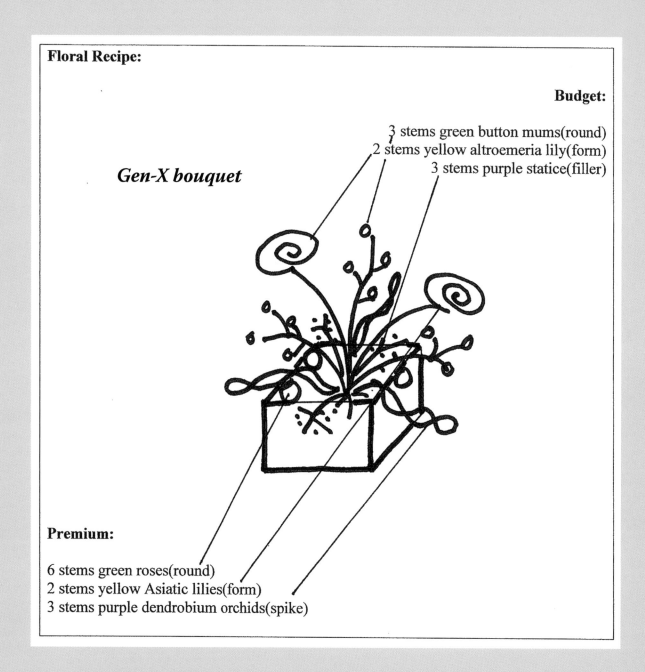

Premium:

6 stems green roses(round)
2 stems yellow Asiatic lilies(form)
3 stems purple dendrobium orchids(spike)

40

Chapter 17 -
"Merry Christmas!" centerpiece

The holidays are a time to celebrate family and friends' enjoying great food and drink, and nothing makes the holiday table feel more special than a festive table centerpiece. Traditional holiday colors are red, green, and gold, although we see many people enjoying non-traditional colors as well. Many cut evergreens such as pine, Frasier, and Noble fir, cedar, and balsam are used in creating the arrangement. Also, candles can be added to illuminate the table with brilliant, flickering light.

Using a low glass bowl or plastic tray, secure a piece of wet floral foam using waterproof tape. Starting with the greens placed around the rim of the container, following the table shape, round or oval. Add additional, shorter greens in the center and accent the arrangement with flowers, pine cones, and ribbons.

Design Tip

Use a hint of gold enamel spray paint on the fern, or some eucalyptus to add an elegant touch to the arrangement.

Floral Recipe:

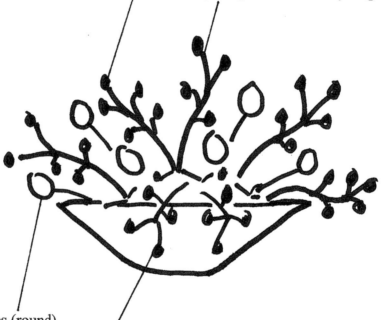

"Merry Christmas!"
centerpiece

Budget:

6 large red carnations (round)
2 sprays white miniature carnations (round)
3 pine cones
3 stems leather leaf
Fresh evergreens
block floral foam cut to fit container
1 rectangular plastic floral tray or glass bowl

Premium:

6 stems red roses (round)
2 sprays white miniature roses (round)
3 holiday ornaments
3 stems eucalyptus
Fresh evergreens
block floral foam cut to fit container
1 rectangular plastic floral tray or glass bowl

Chapter 18 -
Christmas Mantelpiece

Why just decorate the table? Let's have fun and embellish the fireplace mantel, too. Much of the holiday celebrating is spent in the living and family rooms of the house, where the Christmas tree is usually displayed. Most mantels have plenty of space to place an arrangement of evergreens, often accented with candles, pictures, and stockings. The greens are long-lasting and do not require a water source, so you can just place them on top of the mantel.

Cut the bottom limbs from the Christmas tree for your mantel arrangement. Lay the individual pieces with the longer ones extended out and the shorter pieces in the center, stacking the limbs like a shingle roof. Put fresh flowers in water tubes and insert into the greenery; add some pine cones and your favorite ribbon. Family photos, holiday figurines, and candlesticks can be placed in between the evergreen branches.

Design Tip

Add some candy canes to your arrangement during the holidays; the guests can eat and enjoy them.

Flower recipe:

5 stems white snowflake, or cushion spray mums (round)
7 stems red carnations (round)
fresh evergreens
pine cones
12 water tubes
craft wire
ribbon

Premium:

7 stems white snowflake, or cushion spray mums (round)
10 stems red carnations (round)
5 stems orchid sprays(spike)
fresh evergreens
pine cones
22 water tubes
craft wire
ribbon

Christmas Mantelpiece

44

45

Chapter 19 -
The Kris Kringle Wreath

Let jolly old St. Nick greet your guests with a hearty "Ho, ho, ho!" Wire new or heirloom Kris Kringles into a wreath accented with fresh flowers and your favorite ribbon trim. You can display this festive wreath on your front door or above the fireplace mantel. This particular arrangement looks best with traditional colors of red, white, gold, and green, bringing memories of Christmas past back to mind.

Use a permanent or fresh evergreen wreath, and with a light-gauge wire or string, attach the Kris Kringles to the frame. The figures should be in scale with the size of the wreath form. It is recommended that odd numbers be used for focal points on the arrangement: if you are using small figures, add five, medium size add three, and large size use just one or two Kris Kringles. Flowers can be added by placing them in water tubes and wiring them into the wreath.

Design Tip

Weave a red velvet ribbon through the wreath to add traditional charm to this sentimental design.

47

Flower recipe:

The Kris Kringle Wreath

5 stems white snowflake or cushion spray mums (round)
7 stems red carnations (round)
12 water tubes
fresh or permanent wreath
craft wire
ribbon

Premium:

7 stems white snowflake or cushion spray mums (round)
10 stems red carnations (round)
5 stems white orchid sprays (spike)
22 water tubes
fresh or permanent wreath
craft wire
ribbon

Chapter 20 -
Happy Hanukkah centerpiece

Hanukkah is eight days of gift-giving and celebrating. The arrangement can be used to embellish the dining table, coffee table, or buffet table.

The Hanukkah centerpiece consists of primarily blue and white flowers, representing the flag of Israel, accented with candles, festive foliages, and silver trim to reflect Hanukkah's theme as the "Festival of Lights."

Soak the foam in water and wedge it into the container and secure with waterproof tape. Cut and place the flowers into a circular or oval form. Place the fern in between the flowers and add the ribbon treatment. Remember to leave plenty of room on the table for dinnerware. I would recommend placing eight candles, four blue and four white if possible, around the arrangement. If the table is exceptionally long, place four candles at each end of the centerpiece to extend the look and effect.

Design Tip

For some sparkle, add glitter branches or sticks to the design.

Floral recipe:

Happy Hanukkah
centerpiece

Budget:

10 stems white carnations (round)
5 stems white gladioli (spike)
5 stems fern
1 clear plastic or glass bowl
floral foam
blue ribbon

Premium:

10 sprays white orchids (spike)
7 blue delphinium (spike)
10 stems white roses
6 feet blue ribbon
7 stems fern
1 clear plastic or glass bowl
floral foam
blue ribbon

Chapter 21 -
"Happy Halloween" arrangement

Boo! Welcome your favorite hobgoblins with this festive arrangement starring fall's favorite—a pumpkin! Since so many sizes are available in this variety of squash, you can go large, medium, or small, depending on where you are going to use the flowers. For a table arrangement, I would recommend a medium-size pumpkin; if it is going to be placed on the floor, a large pumpkin; and a small size for the window ledge or countertop. Use your favorite variety of fall-colored flowers, which can be accented with some dried flowers. Place a variety of colorful gourds and fall leaves around the base to complete a fall motif.

Simply lop off the top of the pumpkin, scoop out the inside, slip a block of wet floral foam inside, then add your flowers. Work the stems of the fern in between the flowers and add the dried cattails. If you have some freshly raked leaves, add those to the arrangement.

Design Tip

Take cotton, pulled apart to a look like a web, and add plastic spiders for a creepy effect.

Floral recipe:

Budget:

1 pumpkin
5 stems bronze spray mums (round)
5 red carnations (round)
5 stems fern
3 dried cattails (spike)
floral foam cut to fit pumpkin

Premium:

1 pumpkin
5 stems bronze spray mums (round)
5 stems orange lilies (form)
5 red carnations (round)
5 stems fern
3 dried cattails (spike)
floral foam cut to fit pumpkin

"Happy Halloween"
arrangement

Chapter 22 -
"Happy Thanksgiving—Turkey Bouquet"

Gobble! Gobble! No sweating over a hot oven with this "turkey." Here we have a turkey- shaped arrangement that will bring a fun and festive feeling to the table. Creating a novelty design with flowers is as easy as paint-by-numbers, and you can have one or many adorning your table at the holiday dinner. Many of the "ingredients" are right there in your local grocery store—how easy is that?! With these long-lasting flowers, you can create your "turkey" centerpiece several days in advance and enjoy it all through the holiday.

Use one-third block of floral foam in a low tray or cut to fit the container snugly inside. Trim and place the flower heads side-by-side to create a round ball or body of the turkey. To make your turkey bigger, simply add more flowers. You can use mixed-colored mums or roses for a fun look. For the head, use a yellow squash, securing it into the foam with a flower stem or wood pick, and pin two beads or capers for eyes. Cut a piece of red felt or use red pipe cleaners for the turkey's wattle, and pin it to the yellow squash. To fashion a tail, use a piece of palm, fern, or feathers. The turkey can be placed in a low basket or shallow bowl.

Design Tip

Add extra feathers, flowers, or green fern on the sides for wings.

Floral recipe:

*"Happy Thanksgiving—
Turkey Bouquet"*

2 bunches bronze spray mums (round)
1 palm leaf or 5 pieces of fern
1 yellow squash
block floral foam cut to fit container
1 low dish or tray

Premium:

24 orange or fall colored roses fully opened (round)
1 palm leaf or 5 pieces of fern
1 yellow squash
block floral foam cut to fit container
1 low dish or tray

Chapter 23 -
"I Love You" heart-shaped bouquet

Expressions of love should not be exclusive to Valentine's Day. This idea is all about hearts and flowers—and you can combine these two elements to make the perfect present year-round. This gift—a heart-shaped presentation of fresh, fragrant flowers—is ideal for anyone: wife, sister, mother, girlfriend, or significant other. Choose flowers in your sweetheart's color and you will be feeling the love all year long. Red isn't the only color for this special day; use passionate pink or sincere white to express your feelings.

This is an easy one to create! Soak the floral foam heart in water for a minute, then cut the stems of the buds to about two inches and insert them into the floral foam heart until the head of the flower rests on the surface, following the shape of the heart. Keep the flowers close together. Weave the ribbon in between the flower heads.

Design Tip

Place the flower heart in a pretty box for a secretive gift, creating the element of surprise when it is opened.

Floral recipe:

Budget:

"I Love You" heart-shaped bouquet

10 stems pink, red or white miniature carnations (round)
1   5" heart shaped floral foam form
ribbon

Premium:

10 stems pink, red or white spray roses (round)
1   5" heart shaped floral foam form
ribbon

60

Chapter 24 -
"You're so special" Vase Arrangement

No need to worry about calories with this gift! Vase arrangements have been a longtime favorite in the flower markets and florists all across the country, for many reasons. The designs are quick and easy, and the flowers show well in the vases. It is believed that the flowers last better when they are arranged in water, as opposed to floral foam. Often the shape of the arrangement is dictated by the shape of the vase. Straight-edge cylindrical vases create vertical designs, while round bubble-ball vases result in a more rounded arrangement. Whatever your preference, the flowers are beautiful and send the subtle message of love to that special person on Valentine's Day or any time of year.

Fill the vase with water, dry the top, and add a grid of the cellophane tape. (Chapter 2-Mechanics) Waterproof tape will not stick to a surface that is wet or oily. Re-cut the flowers and insert the stems of the flowers through the grid of tape. Remember to lean the ends of the stems against the inside of the vase, so some of the flowers angle out. Add the fern and baby's breath. Use ribbon that matches the flowers, and tie it around the neck of the vase.

Design Tip

Add hearts to the arrangement to express endearing thoughts.

Floral recipe:

Budget:

"You're so special"
Vase Arrangement

1 cello wrapped bunch of mixed
pastel flowers
6 pastel carnations (round)
3 stems baby's breath (filler)
7 stems leather leaf fern
1-8" vase
cellophane tape
ribbon

Premium:

2 bunches of cello wrapped pastel flowers
12 pastel carnations (round)
3 stems baby's breath (filler)
7 stems leather leaf fern
1-8" vase
cellophane tape
ribbon

Chapter 25 -
Happy Mother's Day bubble bowl

A mixture of spring "garden" pastel flowers arranged in a bubble bowl is the perfect way to say "I love you, Mom." Flowers have for a long time been a favorite gift to give Mom on her special day. This is the perfect opportunity to show her how much you care about her and all that she does for you. Taking the extra time and making the effort to create a simple, thoughtful arrangement tells her that she is appreciated. When we think of all that motherhood represents, the flower buds are the perfect gift, signifying new life.

Fill a six-inch bubble bowl container with water and dry the top of the container. Using a twelve-inch-square piece of chicken-wire mesh, fashion a ball to sit on top of the opening, careful not to let it slip inside. (Chapter 2-Mechanics) Starting with the tallest flowers, in the center insert the flowers in between the openings in the mesh, add the greenery and filler flowers. We would suggest that you clean the stems of the greens under water before placing them in the container.

Design Tip

Tie some candy to the flower stems with pretty ribbon for those moms with a sweet tooth.

Floral recipe:

**Happy Mother's
Day bubble bowl**

Budget:

5 stems alsrtroemeria lilies (form)
5 stems carnations (round)
2 stems baby's breath (filler)
6 stems leather leaf fern

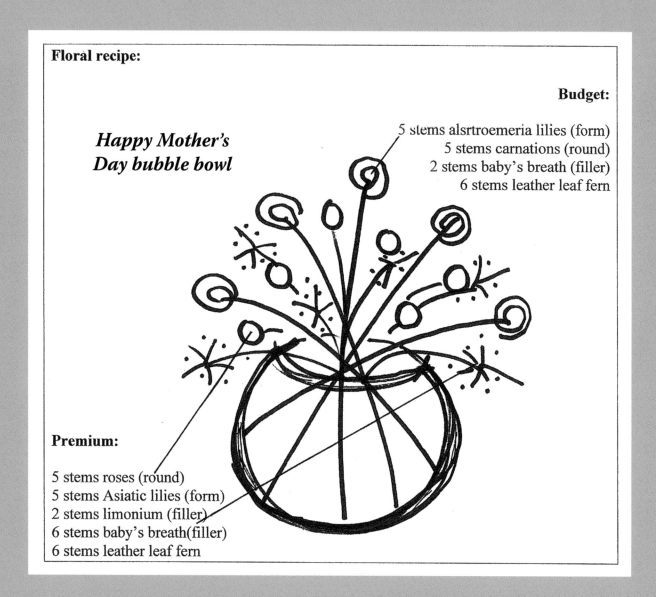

Premium:

5 stems roses (round)
5 stems Asiatic lilies (form)
2 stems limonium (filler)
6 stems baby's breath(filler)
6 stems leather leaf fern

Chapter 26 -
"I'm Worth It!" bouquet

As the saying goes, "If not for me, then for whom? Flowers should not be sent just as expressions to others. Indulge yourself with your favorites. Flowers can and should be enjoyed on a daily basis, since they are so affordable. No need to take a lot of time; just select the colors and varieties that you enjoy most, and arrange them quickly and easily for anyplace in the home or office. As an accent on your desk, coffee table, or even bathroom, these hardy blossoms help us to feel special.

This is an easy and fast arrangement; using a shallow, straight-edged container of any shape, or even a baking dish, shape the wet floral foam to fit tight inside the container about an inch below the rim. Fill with water. Cut the flower stems so the flower heads rest just above the rim of the container. This style is called pave, just like pave diamonds on a piece of jewelry. Doesn't that sound elegant? The flower heads actually hold each other up in the container. You can purchase more flowers to fill in larger containers. Single-stem blossoms work best with this arrangement, such as carnations and roses, because they are hardy and easy to handle.

Design Tip

Create a collar of baby's breath by tucking it around the rim of the container.

Flower recipe:

Budget:

12-24 standard carnations

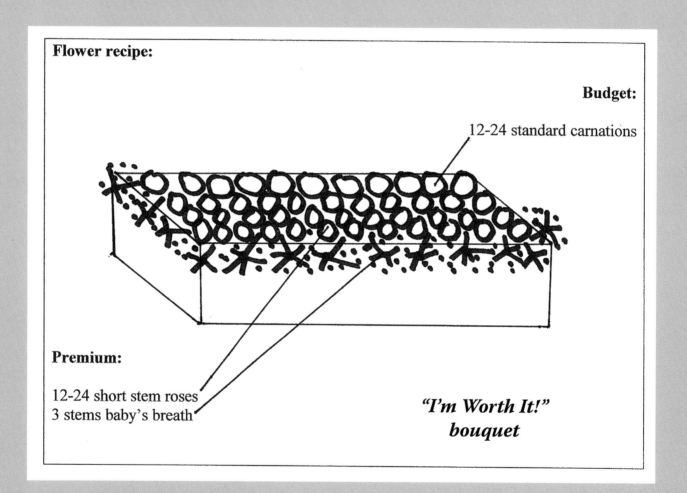

Premium:

12-24 short stem roses
3 stems baby's breath

"I'm Worth It!"
bouquet

Chapter 27 -
"The Subject Was Roses" vase

You can easily create this arrangement in a borrowed vase or splurge on something gorgeous. A dozen long-stemmed roses arranged in a vase is a classy, elegant gift guaranteed to be greeted with "Oohs!" and "Aahs!" Variations on this simple and elegant design can go from a single blossom in a bud vase to many dozens arranged in a large urn, just depending on your budget. Roses are the one flower where color represents feelings. (Chapter 10-Colors of Roses and What They Mean) Although many people purchase and send the colors they like best, we have shared some of the colors and their significant meanings with you.

Select a vase that the roses will easily fit in and the flowers are not overcrowded. I would recommend that you use a vase that is about one-third the length of the rose stems. Fill the container with water and dry the vase. Create a grid with the waterproof tape on the top of the containers. I would recommend that you leave an inch in between the openings of the grid. Placing the tallest roses in the center, cut and insert the roses through the grid into the water. The shorter stems can be placed around the rim of the container, and the ends of the stems can lean against the rounded edge of the vase. Before placing your greens in the arrangement, wash them under water, cut, and add fern and baby's breath between the stems.

Design Tip

Jazz up your arrangement with a variety of fill flowers by mixing baby's breath, limonium, statice, and wax flowers when available.

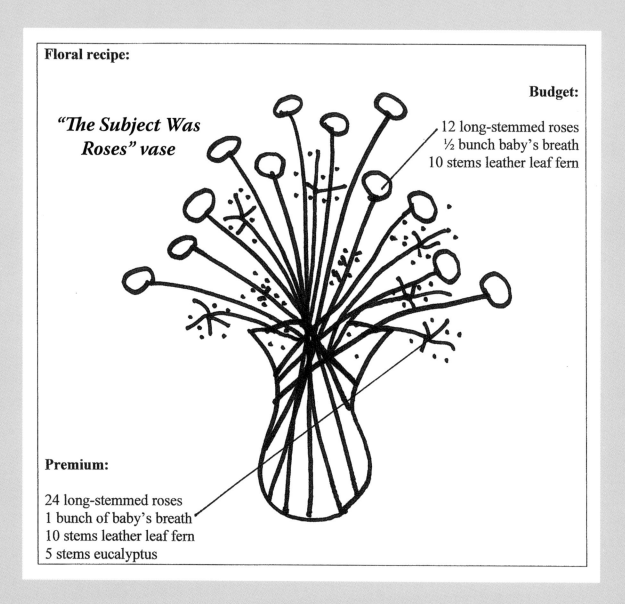

Floral recipe:

"The Subject Was Roses" vase

Budget:

12 long-stemmed roses
½ bunch baby's breath
10 stems leather leaf fern

Premium:

24 long-stemmed roses
1 bunch of baby's breath
10 stems leather leaf fern
5 stems eucalyptus

Chapter 28 -
A Rose Dessert

Here is a fun way to use short- or broken-stem roses: Make a rose dessert for your next dinner party! With so many people watching their weight now, you can have your dessert and eat it too. Truly a feast for the eyes with this fun and clever way to take roses or another favorite flower and dress up the dining table. Place the arrangement into a martini glass or low dessert bowl and use it at each table setting. This will get your guests talking before the first course is served. They can enjoy this visual treat all though the dinner.

Soak the foam sphere in water and cut in half. Cut and place the flower heads side by side to the surface of the foam, completely covering the foam. Place in a pretty bowl or martini glass. Foliage leaves such as lemon leaf or fern can be used under the foam and flowers.

Design Tip

Use the arrangement as a place card holder; just prop the card up in between the flowers.

Floral recipe:
Makes 2 desserts

Budget:

10 stems of white miniature carnations
1 foam sphere cut in half

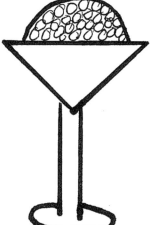

Premium:

10 stems of white spray roses
1 foam sphere cut in half

A Rose Dessert

Chapter 29 -
Happy Easter! Flowers

Nothing says spring like a pot of blooming tulips, and if you don't have a pot of tulip bulbs, you can create the look of one. For the floral design novice, this is a good place to start expressing your talent. The arrangement can be designed in a basket or Easter-themed planter. You can create groupings with a variety of baskets in different sizes. If you decide to use a non-waterproof container, be sure that a liner is placed inside. Add brightly colored eggs at the base and in between the stems of the tulips to complete the motif.

Depending on where you are going to use the arrangement, select the size, style, and shape of your basket. Handles are fun, but make sure that they are secured. Potted tulips are in six-inch grower pots and need a larger basket; when using cut tulips, use a piece of wet floral foam to fit the basket. Cut about one inch from the bottom of the stems and insert into the foam as far as possible. The tulip stems are soft, so do not insert too aggressively. Add green moss or shredded cellophane to the base of the arrangement to cover the soil or floral foam.

Design Tip

Branches of pussy willow and forsythia in fresh or permanent can add an airy look.

Floral recipe:

Happy Easter!
Flowers

Budget:

1 potted tulip or
10 stems of tulips

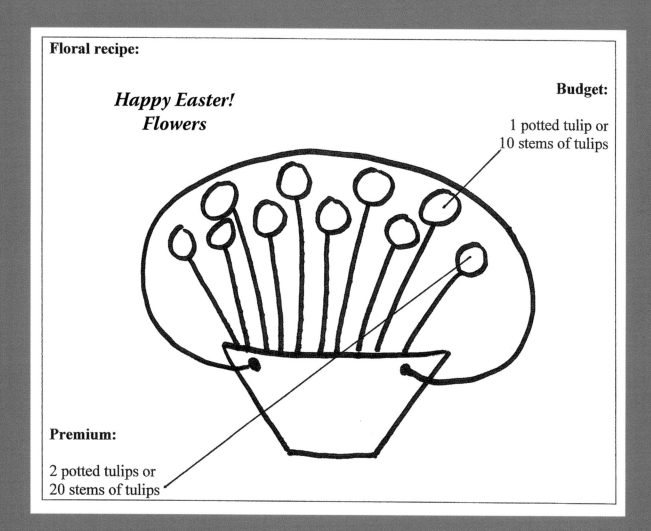

Premium:

2 potted tulips or
20 stems of tulips

Chapter 30 -
Fourth of July Picnic

Watermelon—it's a Fourth of July favorite! And you can use the juicy fruit as the Yankee-Doodle-Dandy centerpiece for your all-American picnic. You won't need any foliage for this arrangement. The melon's rich red color makes a strong statement on its own. Bright primary colors or red, white, and blue are appropriate for this design. You can use one half of the melon for the arrangement and eat the other half by making fruit salad. The flowers easily insert into the natural foam with the water and sugar already in it! Perfect!

After cutting the watermelon in half, re-cut the flowers and insert the stems into the melon as far as possible. Place the tallest flowers approximately fifteen inches in the center of the melon. Shorter stems can be used around the edge of the watermelon and angle out slightly, depending on how much space you have on the tabletop.

Design Tip

Use one or two small American flags in the arrangement for a patriotic look.

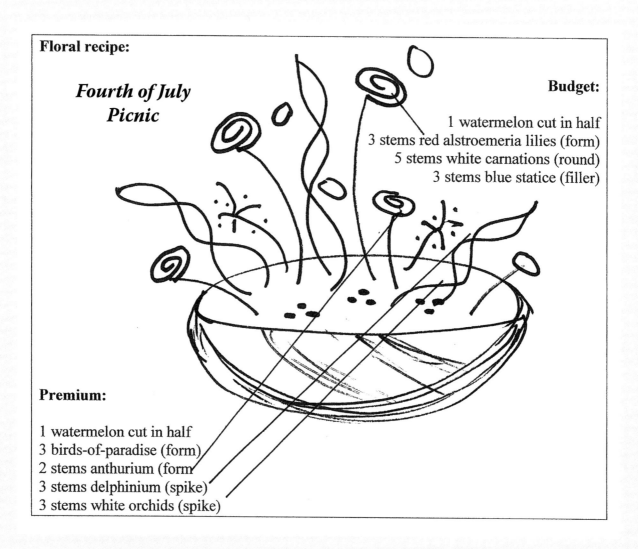

Floral recipe:

Fourth of July
Picnic

Budget:

1 watermelon cut in half
3 stems red alstroemeria lilies (form)
5 stems white carnations (round)
3 stems blue statice (filler)

Premium:

1 watermelon cut in half
3 birds-of-paradise (form)
2 stems anthurium (form)
3 stems delphinium (spike)
3 stems white orchids (spike)

Chapter 31 -
Let's Celebrate Life bouquet

There are celebrations of all types during life, but do we actually celebrate life itself?

Why not? Each day is a victory in many people's lives, so let's acknowledge those small accomplishments with flowers. Whether it is good health, a raise, a promotion, even a divorce marks a turning point in someone's life. You can do it up big or keep it small when recognizing these life-altering happenings. Either way, flowers bring smiles and positive thoughts. I would suggest using an ice or champagne bucket for this arrangement.

Fill the ice or champagne bucket with floral foam just below the rim of the container and add water. Cut the long-stemmed glads and insert those into the center of the floral foam. Add the remaining flowers, inserting into the foam as far as possible. Place the greens low in between the stems to cover the foam.

Design Tip

Use confetti or shredded Styrofoam over the surface of the foam to add color and a motif. Sprinkle more onto the tabletop.

Flower recipe:

Let's Celebrate Life bouquet

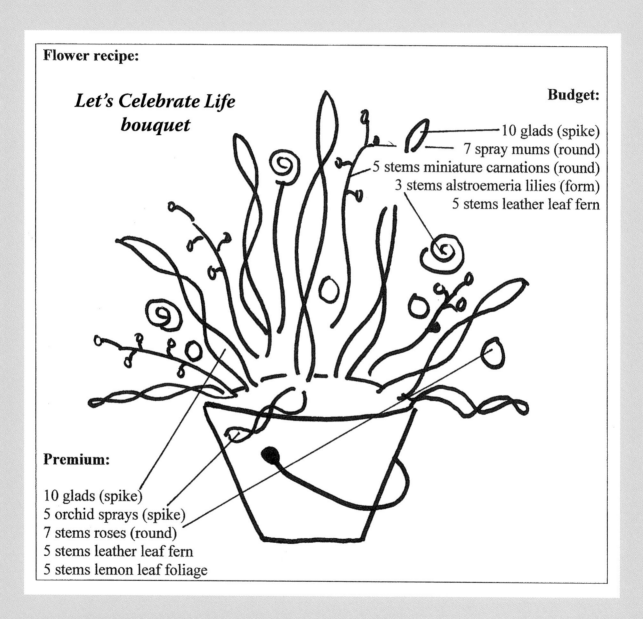

Budget:

10 glads (spike)
7 spray mums (round)
5 stems miniature carnations (round)
3 stems alstroemeria lilies (form)
5 stems leather leaf fern

Premium:

10 glads (spike)
5 orchid sprays (spike)
7 stems roses (round)
5 stems leather leaf fern
5 stems lemon leaf foliage

Chapter 32 -
"I'm Sorry You're Sad" bouquet

There are times when we suffer a loss in our lives—losing a job; the loss of a loved one or even a pet is a sad event, and this is a time when we need the support of our family and friends. Yellow sunflowers are a cheerful color and a casual style flower that bring smiles to us when we need them most. They signify strength when it's needed, but also convey cheerfulness and optimism.

Arrange the sunflowers, two cut tall and three cut lower into a cylinder vase

secured with a taped grid. (Chapter 2-Mechanics) Add the extra flowers at the base of the design. Cut and arrange the lily grass in between the flowers. Add marbles or stones to the base of the arrangement before placing the flowers.

Design Tip

Tie some wooden beads with raffia around the center of the vase.

Floral recipe:

"I'm Sorry You're Sad" bouquet

5 stems sunflowers (round)

Premium:

5 stems sunflowers (round)
5 stems yellow gerbera (round)
1 bunch lily grass

Chapter 33 -
The "O" Birthday Bash

When you mark an "O" birthday—20, 30, 40, 50, 60, 70, 80, 90, or even 100—you're moving from one decade to the next. So celebrate! Go wild with color. Pretend you're a kid again and arrange vibrant primary-colored flowers in a birthday party hat for an extra kick.

To prepare the container, invert the party hat and place a plastic liner or small trash bag inside. Soak a piece of floral foam. Remember, never force the foam under the water. Allow it to soak up water gradually, then place it inside the container and secure it with waterproof tape. When designing with fresh flowers in wet floral foam, insert each stem only once, as far as possible into the wet foam. Removing and reinserting stems weakens the foam. Insert the tallest flowers (spike) into the back portion of the foam to create the arrangement's height and width. Next, insert the medium-stem flowers (round) into the center and side of the foam. Add the filler flowers and fern or lemon leaf in between the stems. To care for it, add water to the top of the container and keep it at room temperature out of direct sunlight.

Design Tip

Festoon the arrangement with horns and ribbons.

Floral Recipe:

Budget:

5-stems red gladioli (spike)

3-stems blue statice (filler)

7-stems red carnations (round)

4-stems yellow daisies (round)

1-deep plastic dish or bowl

block floral foam cut to fit container

birthday hat

5 stems leather leaf fern

The "0" Birthday Bash

Premium:

5-stems blue delphinium (spike)

7-stems red roses (round)

3-stems yellow Asiatic lilies (form)

2-stems baby's breath (filler)

3-stems lemon leaf

1-deep plastic dish or bowl

block floral foam cut to fit container

birthday hat

5-stems leather leaf fern

Chapter 34 -
Everything's "All-White" vase bouquet

White is the absence of color, and reflects light. The flowers are pure elegance and perfect for any setting. When we don't know what a recipient's favorite color is, white is the best choice. Most flowers are also available in white, with the exception of just a few varieties. If the arrangement is going to be used in a dimly lit room, white is the best choice, because the flowers show better. Whatever the occasion and whoever the recipient, you cannot go wrong because it's "All-White."

Start by filling a vase approximately ten inches tall with water. Dry the top and apply a grid, using waterproof tape. Use your spike flowers: gladioli first, and place those in the center of the opening. Second, place the round flowers: roses, in between the spike and allow them to angle out by placing the stem against the inside rounded part of the vase. Balance the arrangement by placing flowers opposite each other. Now you can add the smaller flowers: alstroemeria lily, orchid sprays, and miniature carnations, and finish up with the greens and filler. Remember to keep the vase filled with clean water for maximum flower life.

Design Tip

For a touch of glamour, tie a pretty white wire-edge ribbon around the neck of the vase.

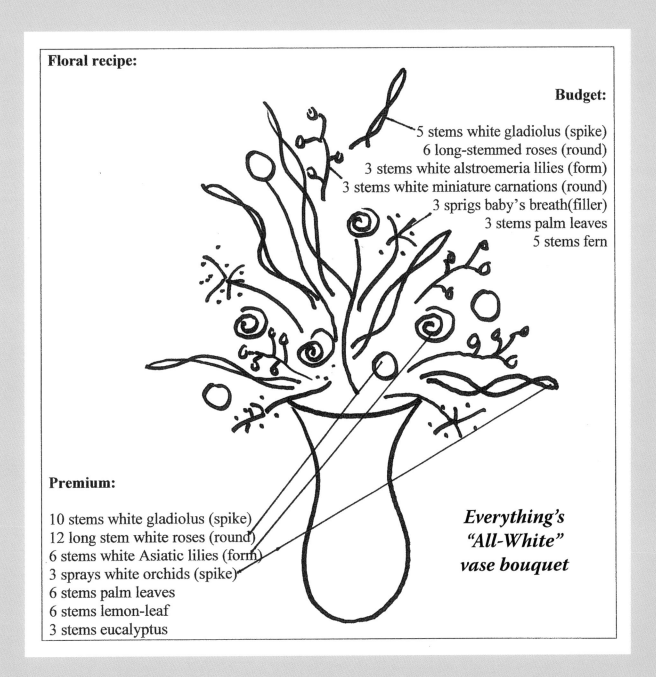

Floral recipe:

Budget:

5 stems white gladiolus (spike)
6 long-stemmed roses (round)
3 stems white alstroemeria lilies (form)
3 stems white miniature carnations (round)
3 sprigs baby's breath(filler)
3 stems palm leaves
5 stems fern

Premium:

10 stems white gladiolus (spike)
12 long stem white roses (round)
6 stems white Asiatic lilies (form)
3 sprays white orchids (spike)
6 stems palm leaves
6 stems lemon-leaf
3 stems eucalyptus

Everything's
"All-White"
vase bouquet

Chapter 35 -
"Bowl Me Over"

Anybody can float flowers in a bowl. Right? Wrong. Flat, round flower forms float best. Gerbera daisies are a great casual flower to float in a bowl. Other "good floaters" are: gardenias, hibiscus, open tulips, anthurium, anemone, and phalaenopsis orchid blossoms. Flowers that do not float: Sunflowers are too heavy, roses tilt, and glads get water-logged. Sometimes we add food coloring or marbles to the water for a dramatic effect. Floating candles can accompany the flowers. Containers that work best are bubble balls, lotus bowls, and cubes. Whatever your choice of flowers and containers, this is a quick and inexpensive way to dress up the dining table.

It's simple to float flowers in a container; just remember to keep enough space in between the blossoms—less is more. Fill the vase with water one-half to three-fourths full or as you prefer; some containers show the flowers better with very little water in them. Remove the entire stem and place the flower on the surface of the water. Having the containers prepared, I would recommend that you do this just before guests arrive for dinner.

Design Tip

Use containers in a variety of sizes and shapes as a grouping in the table center or down the middle of a long table.

Flower recipe:

"Bowl Me Over"

Gerbera daisies or daisy pompons (round)

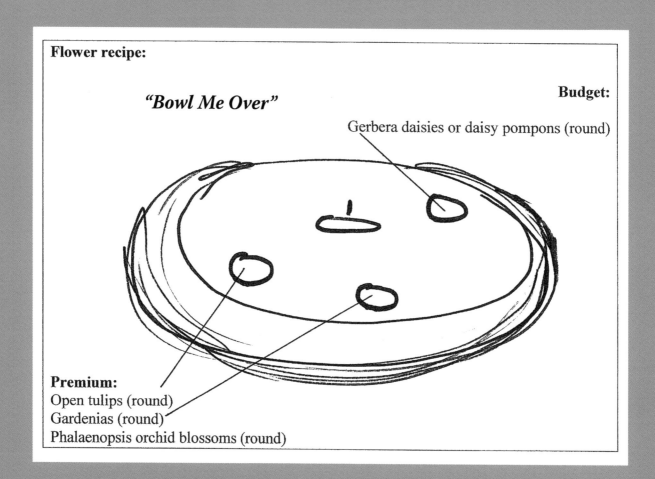

Premium:
Open tulips (round)
Gardenias (round)
Phalaenopsis orchid blossoms (round)

Chapter 36 -
Feng Shui Flowers

An ancient Oriental method of driving good and bad forces, Feng Shui has gained popularity in the United States. Living flowers and plants play a big part in harnessing or altering this beneficial energy, or chi. Flowers placed in an Asian-influenced container at high, medium, and low positions can represent the elements of heaven, man, and earth. This simple design that can be accomplished in just a few minutes brings self-fulfillment and beauty into your living space.

As previously mentioned, use an Asian-influenced container such as a lotus bowl. The flowers are placed into a pin holder also known as a frog or kenzan, which is a metal pad with spikes, used to anchor and secure flowers. The pin holder is simply placed into the container, and the flowers, cut tall, medium, and short lengths, are placed into the pins. The arrangement does not travel well, so, ideally, it should be made where it is going to be finally placed.

Design Tip

Add pebbles and a woven palm leaf for a dramatic look.

Floral recipe:

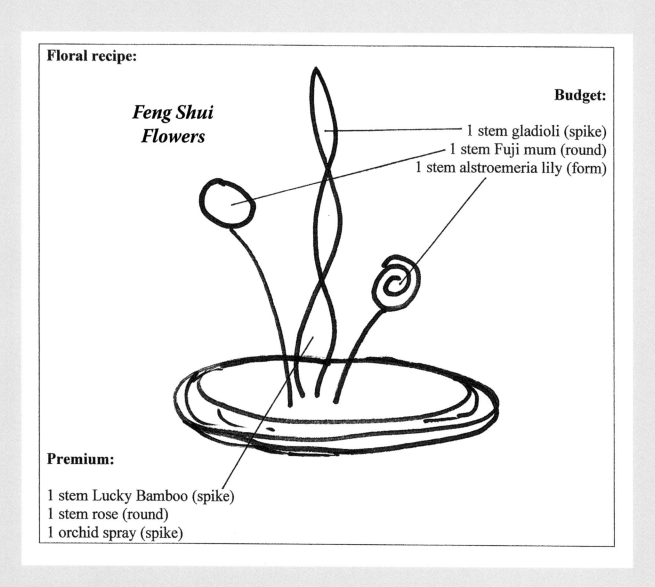

Feng Shui Flowers

1 stem gladioli (spike)
1 stem Fuji mum (round)
1 stem alstroemeria lily (form)

Premium:

1 stem Lucky Bamboo (spike)
1 stem rose (round)
1 orchid spray (spike)

Chapter 37 -
"Orange You Cute!" vase

The citrus color palate is so refreshing! Orange slices placed in a clear glass vase turn a ho-hum container into high-profile centerpieces for just pennies. You can also use lemons or limes, or mix slices of all three citrus fruits for a kicky kaleidoscope of color. With so many selections of clear glass containers available, this idea can be used anywhere. Garden parties are very popular during the spring and summer months, and "Orange You Cute" would be the perfect arrangement for the table center.

The oranges can be used whole as well as sliced; however, inserting the stems in between the slices is easier to accomplish. After the oranges have been placed into the container, fill it with water. Cut and arrange the flowers, inserting the stems as far as possible into the container. Remember, if the arrangement is used as table centerpieces, keep the flowers low enough to see over them.

Design Tip

Skewer fruit such as strawberries or grapes with shish kabob stakes or toothpicks, and place those in between the flowers for added color and texture.

Floral recipe:

"Orange You Cute!"
vase

Budget:

Oranges sliced to fit your container
3 stems white daisies (round)
3 stems yellow daisies (round)
or
2 mixed cello wrapped bunches of flowers

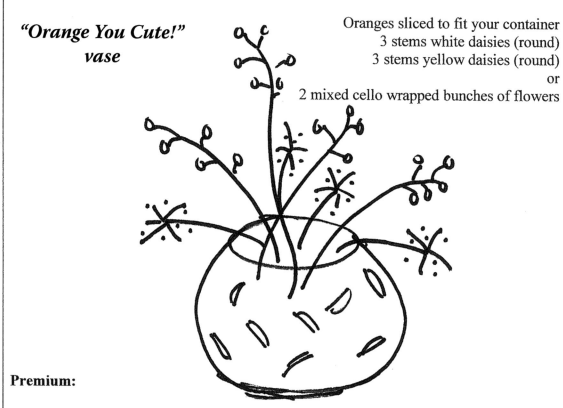

Premium:

Oranges sliced to fit your containers
5 stems white roses (round)
5 stems white miniature carnations (round)
3 springs of baby's breath (filler)

96

Chapter 38 -
Kwanzaa centerpiece

Flowers in bright, bold colors are fitting for this special day of celebration. Centered on traditional African-American values of family, community responsibility, commerce, and self-improvement, Kwanzaa translates as "first fruits of the harvest," and has gained wide acceptance as a national holiday. Candles are important in the Kwanzaa celebration, because fire is a basic element in the universe. Every Kwanzaa celebration includes fire in some form.

Soak the floral foam and secure to the container with waterproof tape. Place the daisies into the arrangement in a triangular position. Cut and add the alstroemeria at varying heights, and place the carnations low into the arrangement. Remember to insert the flower stem as far as possible into the wet foam. Add greenery in between the flower stems. The candles can be used in glass holders and placed about the tabletop around the arrangement.

Design Tip

Use your choice of fruits, nuts, and vegetables, and place those on the table around the centerpiece and candles.

Floral recipe:

*Kwanzaa
centerpiece*

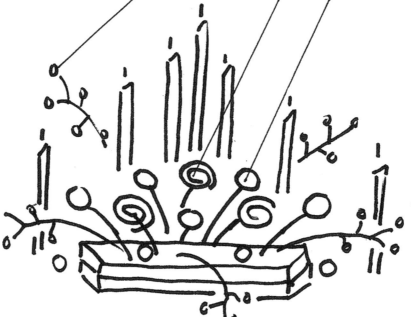

Premium:

5 stems yellow roses (round)
3 stems orange Asiatic lilies (form)
7 stems red carnations (round)
6 stems fern
5 stems palm leaves
floral foam cut to fit container
1 low container
7 candles: 3-red, 3-green, 1-black

Chapter 39 -
Boy's Birthday
Party arrangement

Boys of all ages, young and old, love to celebrate their special day. This is the time to bring their interests into the décor. Toys aren't just for kids anymore! Does your son like trucks? Then use a toy truck as a container. Does your husband like boating? Then use a toy boat as the container. Each motif has endless possibilities just by taking a stroll down the aisle of a toy store. If you idea doesn't work for a container, then add some small items into the design to create a theme. Suggestions we can make are: golf balls, flags, pencils, and pennants. Use flowers in bright primary colors to make a bold statement.

Shape the floral foam to fit snugly inside the chosen container. Remember that if the container is not waterproof, use a plastic

liner such as a garbage bag. Cut and insert the smaller flowers at the top of the arrangement; place the medium-size flowers in the middle, and use the larger flowers at the base. Add fern in between the flower stems.

Party Tip

Research famous people's birthdays for that same day and include that information on the invitation.

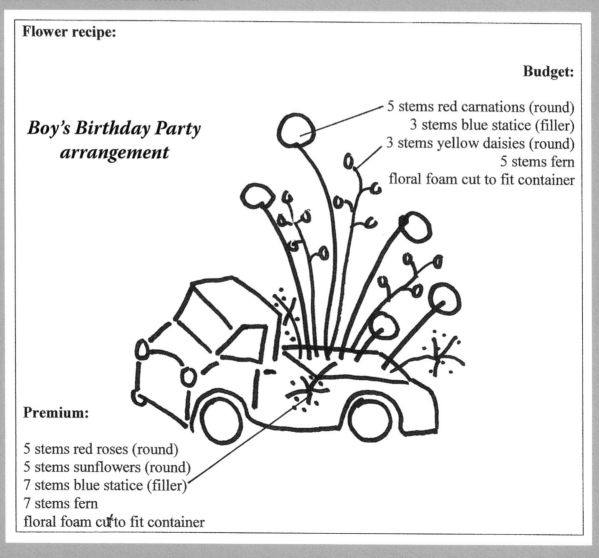

Flower recipe:

Budget:

5 stems red carnations (round)
3 stems blue statice (filler)
3 stems yellow daisies (round)
5 stems fern
floral foam cut to fit container

Boy's Birthday Party arrangement

Premium:

5 stems red roses (round)
5 stems sunflowers (round)
7 stems blue statice (filler)
7 stems fern
floral foam cut to fit container

Chapter 40 -
"Pretty in Pink" Basket

Every little girl loves pink! To make your princess's arrangement even more special, add something personal—and pink—to the basket. Ballet slippers, a favorite stuffed animal, or even a pink-wrapped gift would be perfect. Pink is associated with little girls, so pink flowers are appropriate for this arrangement; maybe even a pink basket.

Cut the floral foam to fit the liner of the basket and soak in water. Place the white flowers first in the center of the basket; arrange the pink flowers around the white. Add greens and baby's breath. If your basket has a handle, be sure to let it show as part of the design. The flowers can be arranged below the handle and angle out the sides.

Design Tip

Add a lace ribbon to the handle of the basket for an additional touch of femininity.

Floral recipe:

"Pretty in Pink" Basket

Budget:

5 pink carnations (round)
5 white carnations (round)
2 stems baby's breath (filler)
5 stems fern
handled basket
floral foam cut to fit container

Premium:

5 pink roses (round)
5 white roses (round)
4 stems baby's breath (filler)
5 stems fern
handled basket
floral foam cut to fit container

Chapter 41 -
Ladies' Tea Party arrangement

Flowers for the afternoon tea create a special moment when stories and peaceful times are shared. Use your favorite cups and saucers as containers for an afternoon tea. Since the containers are small, the arrangements will only require a few dainty buds. The colors can match the containers, or they can be soft pastels accented with baby's breath and ivy. The choices are yours, and since the occasion is only a few hours long, buds that last a short time will do just fine.

Trim the floral foam to fit snugly into the teacup, and fill with water. I would recommend adding the foliage or, if you are using a hydrangea blossom divided, first.

Inserting the stems as far as possible into the foam next, add the remaining flowers. The foliages can peek out from behind the flowers; remember not to cover up your teacup.

Design Tip

Group three or five cups and saucers on a tray for a lovely centerpiece, and they make great gifts for your guests to take home.

Floral recipe:

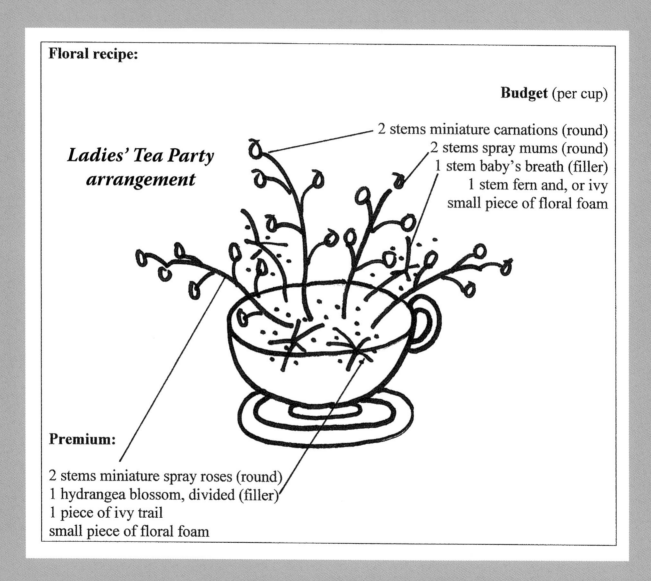

Budget (per cup)

2 stems miniature carnations (round)
2 stems spray mums (round)
1 stem baby's breath (filler)
1 stem fern and, or ivy
small piece of floral foam

*Ladies' Tea Party
arrangement*

Premium:

2 stems miniature spray roses (round)
1 hydrangea blossom, divided (filler)
1 piece of ivy trail
small piece of floral foam

Chapter 42 -
Book Club centerpiece

Book clubs are becoming more and more popular as a way to get friends who are passionate about reading together. It's easy to create a flower arrangement if the book you are reading is about flowers, like **The Frugal Florist,** but if not, you can still follow the theme of your book club's reading choice to create a conversation-stimulating centerpiece. Simply prop up your book to create a focal point for your tabletop arrangement. Here's an arrangement idea for the classic novel **To Kill a Mockingbird.**

Soak the floral foam in water and attach to the dish with waterproof tape. Cut and insert the daisies into the back of the floral foam as deep as possible. Remember, removing and reinserting stems weakens the foam. Next, add the carnations and greens in between the flowers. Tuck the bird nests and birds in between the flower stems and on top of the greens. Prop up the book and place it next to the arrangement.

Design Tip

Add branches or other elements to unite the theme of the arrangement and create harmony.

Floral recipe:

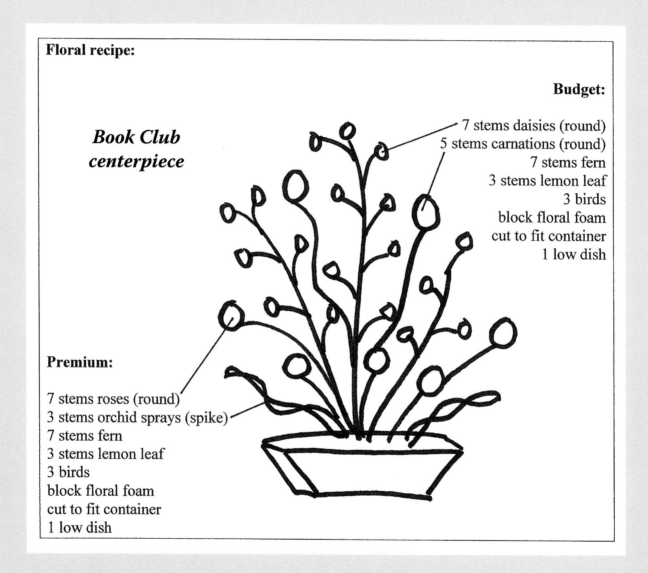

Book Club centerpiece

Budget:

7 stems daisies (round)
5 stems carnations (round)
7 stems fern
3 stems lemon leaf
3 birds
block floral foam
cut to fit container
1 low dish

Premium:

7 stems roses (round)
3 stems orchid sprays (spike)
7 stems fern
3 stems lemon leaf
3 birds
block floral foam
cut to fit container
1 low dish

Chapter 43 -
Graduation Day arrangement

Every graduation marks a milestone—whether it's kindergarten or college or something in between. Graduation marks the start of a new beginning, so bold, bright flowers, possibly tropical, are the ideal combination to celebrate a new start. Accent the design with the graduate's diploma, mortar board and tassel, or favorite school photos.

Start by soaking the floral foam for a few minutes and attach it to the container with waterproof tape. Cut the flowers on an angle and place the taller spike flowers in the center of the foam as deep as possible and allow them to angle out slightly. Remember not to remove and reinsert, as this weakens the foam. Next, insert the round flowers and add the lilies to the base. Add the greens in between the flowers last. You can place the arrangement behind or beside the framed diploma and photos of the graduate.

Design Tip

Attach the tassel to a flower stem and let it hang down into the arrangement.

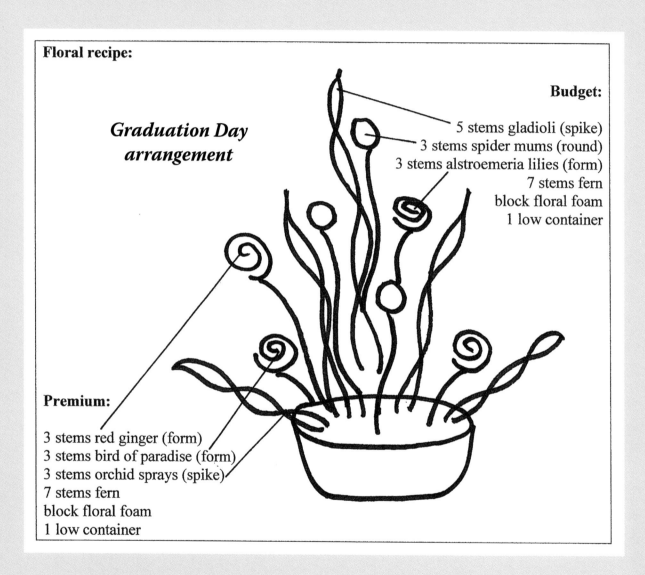

Floral recipe:

Graduation Day arrangement

Budget:

5 stems gladioli (spike)
3 stems spider mums (round)
3 stems alstroemeria lilies (form)
7 stems fern
block floral foam
1 low container

Premium:

3 stems red ginger (form)
3 stems bird of paradise (form)
3 stems orchid sprays (spike)
7 stems fern
block floral foam
1 low container

Chapter 44 -
"I'm Proud to Be an American" wreath

Show your true colors on Presidents' Day, Memorial Day, Veteran's Day, Flag Day, and the Fourth of July by hanging this colorful red-white-and-blue-themed wreath on your front door. Displayed with the American flag, this patriotic arrangement shows your proud support for our many men and women who have served and continue to serve our country.

Soak the floral foam wreath form in water for two minutes and allow it to drain. Cut small pieces of greens and insert into the floral foam, covering the form as much as possible, adding more foliage if needed. Cut the white flowers' stems to three inches and insert them into the floral foam as deep as possible. Repeat with the red and blue, placing the flower colors evenly around the wreath form. Add the flags and pin in the ribbon. The wreath can be hung with a hanger, nail, or placed flat on a tabletop for a centerpiece.

Design Tip

This arrangement can be duplicated in silk flowers using a Styrofoam wreath form.

Floral recipe:

Budget:
10 stems red carnations (round)
5 stems baby's breath (filler)
5 stems blue statice (filler)
10 stems fern
3 small flags
8" floral foam wreath ring
red-white-blue ribbon (optional)

Premium:

10 stems red carnations (round)
10 stems white carnations (round)
7 stems blue statice (filler)
10 stems fern
3 strands ivy
3 small flags
8" floral foam wreath ring
red-white-blue ribbon (optional)

*"I'm Proud
to Be an
American"
wreath*

Chapter 45 -
Happy New Year centerpiece

Celebrating the holidays is great fun, sharing time, food, and gifts with family and friends. The New Year's baby marks a time of new beginnings and saying good-bye to Father Time. Welcome in the New Year by creating a tabletop arrangement of dramatic white, black, and silver, maybe utilizing a plastic silver container. A champagne bucket is ideal.

Cut the floral foam to fit snugly into your container and fill with water. Start with

the Fiji or spider mums, and insert those stems deep into the floral foam. Next, add the carnations or roses, angling out of the arrangement. Add greens and miniature carnations or orchid sprays to the base of the design. Weave the black ribbon through the stems of the flowers and let it spill out onto the tabletop.

Design Tip

Add sparkle to the arrangement by inserting glittered sticks, dried pods or branches into the foam.

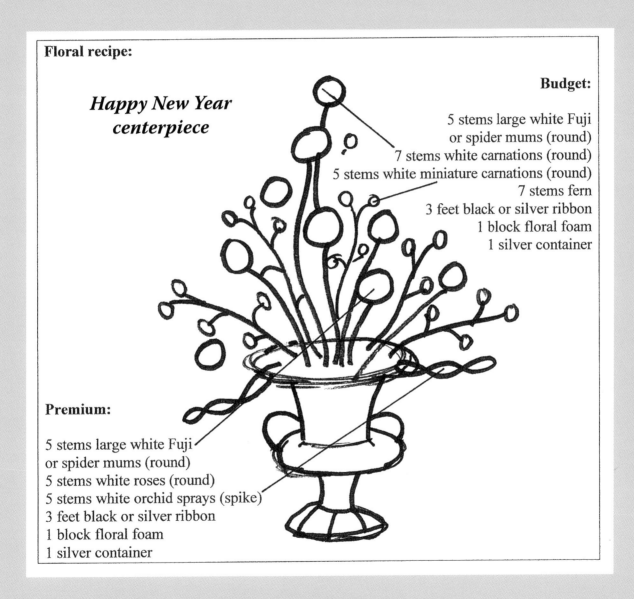

Floral recipe:

Happy New Year centerpiece

Budget:

5 stems large white Fuji
or spider mums (round)
7 stems white carnations (round)
5 stems white miniature carnations (round)
7 stems fern
3 feet black or silver ribbon
1 block floral foam
1 silver container

Premium:

5 stems large white Fuji
or spider mums (round)
5 stems white roses (round)
5 stems white orchid sprays (spike)
3 feet black or silver ribbon
1 block floral foam
1 silver container

Chapter 46 -
Lousy Weather bouquet

Rainy, snowy, bleak days always get you down, so if you're feeling blue, give yourself a calorie-free lift! Yellow evokes happiness, and a bouquet of all yellow flowers is guaranteed to bring a smile to your face. You say you don't have time for light therapy? Well then, this is the alternative. A bright bouquet of yellows and greens in your favorite basket brings sunshine to your office or home, and aren't you worth it?

I would recommend using a basket with a least an eight-inch opening. If a liner is not available, you can use a garbage bag inside to make it waterproof. Secure the foam with waterproof tape or a wire over the top of the foam and worked through the weave of the basket. Cut and place the smaller flowers first into the floral foam. Remember to insert as deep as possible. Next, add the mid-size flowers, such as alstroemeria or roses, and last, add the large sunflowers near the base of the basket; now place your greens into the foam. If you are using any filler such as yellow aster or baby's breath, add that last. Keep the basket filled with water and away from a heater, as this will dry out the flowers.

Design Tip

Bring the elements of nature into your home or office by adding artificial butterflies to the arrangement.

Floral recipe:

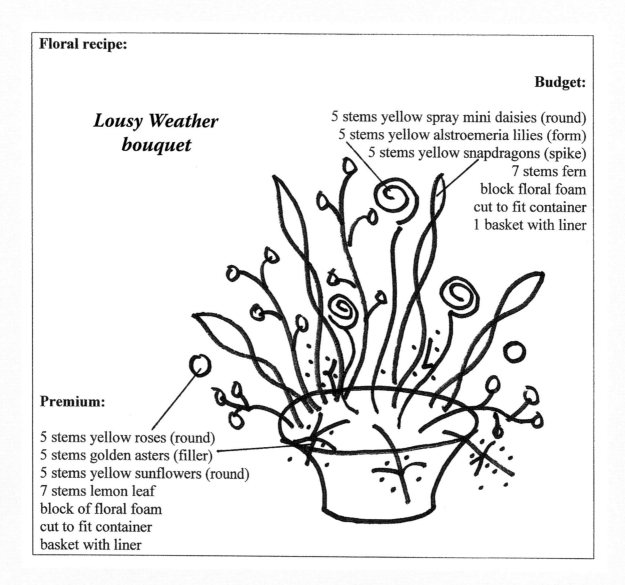

Lousy Weather bouquet

Budget:

5 stems yellow spray mini daisies (round)
5 stems yellow alstroemeria lilies (form)
5 stems yellow snapdragons (spike)
7 stems fern
block floral foam
cut to fit container
1 basket with liner

Premium:

5 stems yellow roses (round)
5 stems golden asters (filler)
5 stems yellow sunflowers (round)
7 stems lemon leaf
block of floral foam
cut to fit container
basket with liner

Chapter 47 -
"Thank-You" mug

An office colleague, employee, or your child's teacher will appreciate this arrangement of bright buds in a coffee mug. You can say "thanks" in many languages, and the flowers speak them all. I would suggest that you pick up a mug at the store while shopping for your flowers. Use a complementary-colored mug that contrasts with the flowers. For example: blue mug-orange flowers, yellow mug-lavender flowers, green mug-red flowers. You can reference the color wheel (Chapter 6-Use of Color) for other options; just look for colors opposite each other.

Cut the floral foam to fit snugly inside the mug. I would recommend that the arrangement be twice the height of the mug. Re-cut and insert the small flowers first into the foam as deep possible. Next, add the midsize flowers, roses or carnations, in the center, and add the greens and baby's breath last.

Design Tip

Tuck pencils, pens, and a small notepad in between the flower stems.

Floral recipe:

"Thank-You" mug

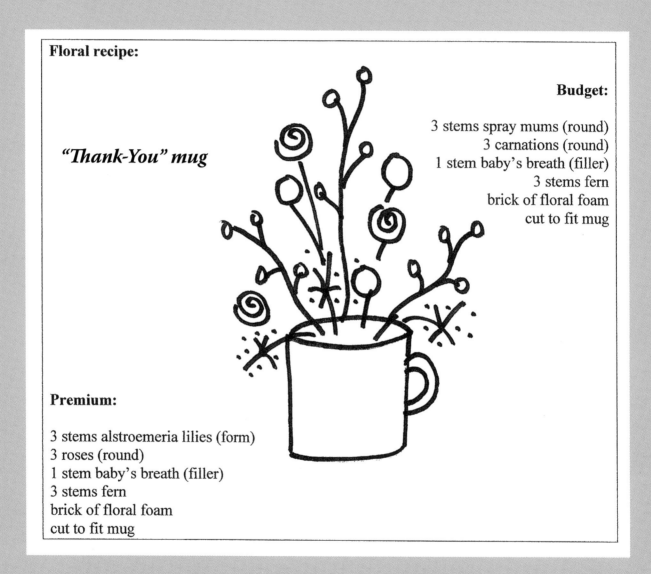

Budget:

3 stems spray mums (round)
3 carnations (round)
1 stem baby's breath (filler)
3 stems fern
brick of floral foam
cut to fit mug

Premium:

3 stems alstroemeria lilies (form)
3 roses (round)
1 stem baby's breath (filler)
3 stems fern
brick of floral foam
cut to fit mug

Floral recipe:

"Go Team"
Tailgate picnic

Budget:

2 bunches of cello wrapped
fall colored mixed flowers
or
10 stems red carnations (round)
5 stems yellow daisies (round)
10 stems leather leaf fern
1 block floral foam
cut to fit container

Premium:

10 stems red roses (round)
3 stems yellow Asiatic lilies (form)
10 stems leather leaf fern
1 block of floral foam
cut to fit container

Chapter 48 -
"Go Team" Tailgate picnic

Rah! Rah! If you're a football fan, build a centerpiece around a pigskin for a tailgate party. It might be a challenge to find a football container, so if one is not available, use a small picnic basket or beer cooler. I would recommend that you choose flowers in your favorite team colors and place the pennant in or near the arrangement.

Soak the floral foam for two minutes and cut it to fit your container. If you are using a picnic basket, place the foam in a waterproof container (cut a water or bleach bottle in half), and secure with waterproof tape. Cut and insert into the foam as far as possible the smaller flowers first, starting at the top. I would recommend making the arrangement two times the height of your container. Add the medium-size flowers and ferns to cover the floral foam.

Design Tip

Accent the arrangement with some dried fall leaves.

Chapter 49 -
Gladioli Towers

Simple gladioli are one of our most elegant, versatile flowers. These are typically cut and dropped into a flared vase for the dining or coffee table. Now you can create towers of glads to be used in groupings or lined up in a row to create drama. One of nature's most colorful and affordable flowers, gladioli are not just for funerals anymore! Mix and match the colors or keep the color scheme monochromatic; either way, you can create a stunning effect with these dynamic blooms.

You can use one long container or several small containers, such as cocktail glasses. If you use deep containers such as terra cotta pots, put a liner inside. Glass cubes would also be ideal for this project. The colored floral foam (purchased at <u>www.frugalflorist.biz</u>) can be cut to fit and wedged into the container about an inch below the rim, so waterproof tape isn't needed. Remember, allow up to 5 minutes for the colored foam to soak. Cut approximately two inches from the bottom of the stem on an angle and insert into the floral foam as far as possible. Remember to keep the stems in a straight vertical line. Add as many stems to the container as you wish or as many as will fit.

Design Tip

Cover the floral foam with moss, colored marbles, beads, or crystals.

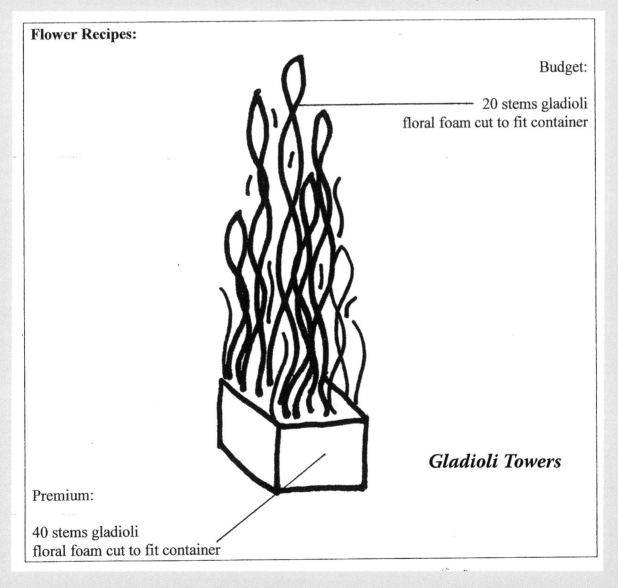

Flower Recipes:

Budget:

20 stems gladioli
floral foam cut to fit container

Gladioli Towers

Premium:

40 stems gladioli
floral foam cut to fit container

Chapter 50 -
Happy Sweet 16 Birthday cake

Sweet Sixteen is truly a special moment in a young girl's life as she approaches adulthood. In the Spanish culture Quinceañera or *Quince Años* (sometimes represented *XV Años*, meaning "fifteen years"). You can create excitement with bright, fun flowers in mixed colors or stay with a monochromatic (shades, tints, and tones of the same hue) color scheme. Accent the top of the flower cake with a number 16 candle or whatever number is appropriate. You can also add additional birthday candles on the cake top. Whatever you decide to do, have fun with this easy and simple arrangement.

Soak the floral cake form in water for about two minutes and place on a shallow tray, allowing it to drain. Cut the flowers, leaving about one inch of stem, and insert the flower heads into the surface of the floral foam. Follow the shape of the form and keep the flowers close to each other, completely covering the foam form. Circle the base of the cake with pieces of fern.

Design Tip

Place the cake on a fancy cake plate in the table center. Sprinkle the cake top and table with confetti or flower petals.

Flower recipe

Happy Sweet 16
Birthday cake

Budget:

For a mixed colored cake:
use approximate 4 bunches
of mixed cello wrapped flowers
3 stems fern

For a solid color cake:
Use 5-6 bunches of miniature carnations
3 stems fern

Premium:

Use 5-6 bunches of spray roses
3 stems fern